Kangaroos
in the
Land Down Under

Shelby Braidich

Rosen Classroom Books & Materials
New York

Published in 2003 by The Rosen Publishing Group, Inc.
29 East 21st Street, New York, NY 10010

Copyright © 2003 by The Rosen Publishing Group, Inc.

Book Design: Haley Wilson

Photo Credits: Cover, p. 1 © SuperStock; pp. 6-7, 12, 14 © Fritz Prenzel/Animals Animals; p. 4 © Tecmap Corporation; Eric Curry/Corbis; p. 8 (top) © Ken G. Preston-Mafham/Animals Animals; p. 8 (bottom) © Tim Tuten/Animals Animals; p. 11 © David Fritts/Animals Animals.

ISBN: 0-8239-6371-3
6-pack ISBN: 0-8239-9553-4

Manufactured in the United States of America

CPSIA Compliance Information: Batch #WR016180RC:
For Further Information contact Rosen Publishing, New York, New York at 1-800-237-9932

Contents

Equator

AUSTRALIA

"The Land Down Under"

Australia (aw-STRAYL-yuh) is the sixth largest country in the world. It is the only country that is also a **continent**. Most of Australia is hot and dry. Few people live far **inland**, away from the oceans. Australia is called "The Land Down Under" because it is the only continent completely below the **equator** (ee-KWAY-tuhr).

◀ People in Australia live mainly on the coasts near the water, where it is usually warm and sunny.

Kangaroos

Kangaroos are furry animals that live in Australia. Kangaroos have long back legs and feet. Some kangaroos can hop faster than thirty miles an hour and can jump twenty-five feet or more! Kangaroos guard themselves from enemies and other kangaroos by kicking with their back legs. Kangaroos use their short front legs to walk and to hold things.

◀ Kangaroos have long, powerful tails. They use their tails to balance themselves when leaping, walking, and fighting.

gray kangaroo

red kangaroo

Two Types of Kangaroos

There are two common types of kangaroos. Gray kangaroos live in the forests and **grasslands** of southern and eastern Australia.

Red kangaroos are often larger than gray kangaroos. They live in the hot deserts and grasslands in the middle of Australia. Male red kangaroos can grow to be six feet tall and weigh up to 200 pounds.

◀ Gray and red kangaroos both eat grass and small plants. Both can live for months without drinking water.

Kangaroo Families

Kangaroos live in groups called **mobs**. Mobs often have around twelve kangaroos, but may have more. For each male kangaroo, or "boomer," there are about five females, or "flyers." Young kangaroos are called "joeys." Joeys spend their days playing, sleeping, and eating.

Since it is hot in Australia most of the time, ▶ kangaroo mobs often spend the day resting. They search for food at night, when it is cooler.

Baby Kangaroos

Mother kangaroos give birth to babies that have not finished **developing**. Newborn joeys are about the size of a jelly bean! Joeys finish developing in a **pouch** on their mother's belly. When the joey is about six to eight months old, it leaves its mother's pouch and moves around by itself.

◄ Newborn joeys don't have fur for the first three months of their lives. They don't open their eyes for the first four months.

Kangaroos and People

In recent years, there have been too many kangaroos in Australia. The government lets some farmers hunt large kangaroos that destroy crops. Some farmers are allowed to hunt a few kangaroos for food and for their skins, which are made into leather. Kangaroos are very special animals in Australia, so they are hunted only when necessary.

Glossary

continent   One of the seven great bodies of land on Earth.

develop   To grow.

equator   An imaginary line around the middle of Earth that separates it into two parts, north and south.

grassland   Flat, dry land covered with grasses and small plants.

inland   The inside area of a country or island that is far away from the coasts.

mob   A group of kangaroos.

pouch   A sack on a mother kangaroo's belly used to carry baby kangaroos.

Index